POEMS
OF
A
MANIC DEPRESSIVE

BY

JUDITH MAIMAN

POEMS
OF A
MANIC DEPRESSIVE
BY
JUDITH MAIMAN

PUBLISHED
BY
LONE OAK PRESS, LTD.
304 11th AVENUE SE
ROCHESTER, MINNESOTA
55904
507-280-6557

**ILLUSTRATED
BY
LOU FERRERI**

ISBN NUMBER 0-9627860-4-7

CONTENTS

Dedicated to Justin

with special thanks to Anne Muellerleile
and
Dr. Terri Atkinson

My Child is Like a River

Justin scramble
Justin tumble
Justin run.
When I was long and lovely
you were born.

O run now, cascade
the rocks hollowing
hollering run.
There is no belief like blue.
My students hover round
me. Shape, form, I tell
them.
Like Justin run.

Alzheimers

Blueberry pancake lady,
I remember you.
You carved a broken promise
out of only the best
of wood, of music, of laughter.

In my youth,
you crafted me, traded me,
blew me into the future.
Now you can't remember
my name.
You led me through
rooms of alabaster, Persian
rugs where we drank
cointreau.

So you swagger into the
space waving your arms.
What is going on.
Who are you.
Would we could go back
to that gentle pond
where we gathered cattails.

To A Sister

My one time sister.
Master of hangings.
You translated art from soul,
a protein studded star.
You were September time to
me in a house I wanted
to create.
Your movements classical.
Your orbit full.

How many times I never
loved you perfect
like a sound heard once,
like the name Brianna.

I was contained by you.
I was another thought
you had sparkle quick
in you life.
You designed.
You inspired.
It was a gift arms out.

The Psychiatric Ward

Wrap your head
in thorazine,
like a band aid,
like a crown of thorns.
If you thought
you were the messiah,
they will take away
your feelings.

You are nothing special
in the psyche ward.
You are manic-depressive.
You do the thorazine shuffle.
Walls inhibit you,
and of course
the lock on the door.

For you who brought
something unique
into the world
are now a mass of neurons.
Psychotropic drugs
will soon take them over.

Laughter is banned
from the psyche ward.
What's funny about
a broken brain?

There are occupational therapists
who smile
like little wind up dolls.
But it doesn't help remove
the dread.

Depression hits
like ice sticking to
a pavement.
Gone are the days of drinking.

Gone are the days of independence.
Self esteem makes
a blind attempt
and fails.

We are pieces of driftwood
abandoned on the shore,
sticking out all over
smoothed by the medication.
The water washes over us.
We are at its mercy.
The mercy of Doctors,
nurses and Psychiatrists.

Out the barred windows
is resurrection for some.
The sky is blue.
Spring has coaxed
buds out of the trees.
There are pastures
with sleek Arabian horses.
I will gallup to freedom.

The Treatment

1000 milligrams of thorazine
pulled me down into the
pillow.
It was a death.
The lack of air brought me
back to life
hyperventilating.

They sent me the nurse
with red hair
who watched me rip off
my nightgown and bra.

The next morning
I dressed and walked
like a zombie,
the baby I was crying
about yesterday, forgotten.

That thorazine worked perfectly.
I had no feelings, no ideas.
I was no trouble to anyone.
My mind couldn't wander
into the absurd.
Every secretion of my brain
had been altered.
No personality.
No self.

Mania

Four months ago
I had Tardive Disknesia.
The Doctor changed
my medication from
a major tranquilizer
to a narcotic and
I began to feel after
15 years.

Sprawled out in the chair .
Do I dare disturb the
universe?
I began to explain.
So you see Dr. Chastek,
I was manic.
Detail after detail
I told him.

Manic is that big word.
Like incandescent,
surreptitious, anonymous.
It can't be small like
gay happy pretty.
Manic is when you buy
Safari perfume.

And he said--
Listen to what he said
very carefully:
"Judy you were just happy"
You were just goddamned
happy.

Happiness was a time
when I was pregnant.
In those days I used
to take my broken belly
into the woods,
photographing dead trees.
I was the artist
and the forest provided
sculptures for me.

There was burnt sienna
and azure and yellow ochre.
My blood pressure was high.
The doctor must have
taken it 50 times.

Illness I

Changing from a
major tranquilizer
to a minor one,
is like slipping
down a slope
too fast.
The skis don't know
which way to point
and the trees make
very bad markers.

Emotions which for
years have lain
dormant suddenly
overwhelm the ego.
Too much dopamine.

I wanted an angel
beside me to say
"this is appropriate,
and that is not."
I wanted a thousand
revisions, a thousand
ways to say, "I'm hungry."

Desire shot out of the
woods like a wolf
nipping at my heels.
I wanted the skis
to dance in the snow.
I wanted my poems
to be the best.
I wanted sex, speed,
pleasure.

And all the time
the cat purred in my lap,
saying you haven't
changed. You still
scratch my
back. You still sit
on the couch. You
still get dressed
every morning.

What is that hard core
at our center.
That being that beats
the time we take.

The cat disappears.
The angel disappears.
The ski slope is far away.
There is no pleasure here.
I am alone.

Social Security

The progression
was something like this,
6 weeks hospital
10 years marriage
20 years work
Social Security Disability.

Debbie called.
She works for Social Security.
She said "They
determined that you
are disabled."
The word hit me like
a hard ball,
like a thunderstorm,
like a bunch of
kids pulling at my coat.

Define your terms
I wanted to say.
Let's not use that
nasty word.

I am disenchanted,
dissatisfied, disturbed
confused, "off my
rocker," crazy, but not
disabled even though
it means $7000 back
pay.

In the old days
war had heroes
and some of them
were disabled. I
have no proof
no reason
no justification.

Illness II

Outside my apartment
sits the Bronco II
which will take me
to suburbia.

In my son's car
lies the map
that will show me
the way to Ely
and the Boundary Waters.

On my mahogany table
sits the white phone.
I can make reservations
to Italy.

Too many employment pages.
Too many possessions.

Or did I forget.
I'm Manic Depressive.
I'm hooked to my psychiatrist.
What about panic attacks
in the canoe.
911 in Italy.

I am confined to a wheel chair.

Italy

Nine months in Italy.
Fifteen blonde Americans.
They called us whores
because we stayed
up after 10.

That was not the
American sky I
saw in Italy.
The light was
more diffuse,
more painterly.

Down from the windows
next to our pensione
came baskets on a rope
filled with bazaar goods.
In Italy its no
excuse to be a peasant.

To be moved by
Italians who love you.
In Positano,
Sergio and I explored
the houses dotting
the hillside.
Once the hillside
was my protection.
Sergio had a knife
and I was a virgin.

But the sea

the savior the sea
was at the bottom
of all those
postcard houses
fronted with flowers.

The sea answered
questions from my
youth.
The sea, meeting the
horizon at the point of God.

Dué jouné fa
was the Italian
version of "a Man and
a Woman." Music
translated from
the American was
popular, sounding
much better in
Italian to us
who cherished every
Italian moment.

Feet walking on
narrow streets
where every building
had a color.
Sidewalk cafés on
the Via Veneto.
We drank and watched.

At Hirculaneum
the fresco was
unfinished,
and the archaeologists
gone so we
picked up pieces
of angel heads
and women.

My Father The Doctor

The Chief of Staff
at the hospital
had hands.
He had hands that
stitched around any
wounds.
He could have been
a musician,
those hands
on a trumpet.

He brought so many
babies out of the
womb into the real
world.
Was he the first one
they saw?
Out of that precious
liquid. Out of all
protection. The
greatest freedom.

At home those hands
grabbed for the shot glass,
the valium.
Years later he was to
tell me that he
almost lost his
medical license.
He was crying.
Years later I was to
tell him I never
had a father.

Yet he had that mind.
That cerebral magnificence.
A cellular renegade,
reading the Atlantic
the New Yorker and
The Smithsonian.
I always respected him.
We make excuses for
genius.

Parable

This is the story of one man.
This is the story of two women.
One beloved for eternity.
The other chained and scarred
with several pieces of joy.

The one is older and dowdy.
She has no pretense,
and he clutches her like
one would fondle an old teddy bear.
The other is good for sex.
He has some feelings for her.

Juggling two women is hard
he says.
Hard for who?
I would like to juggle two men
but I don't know how to juggle.

They don't share the same fate,
the three of them.
It's a puzzle.

Sara will go to far away lands
where bazaars glitter
with black market goods,
and men pee in the street.
She will sweep the dirt floor daily
an empty the ash trays.
She will ride an Arabian horse
that is uncontrollable.
She is scared.

Julia will stay at home
writing poetry.
Women poets are too smart.
Julia carries the pain of this story.
She rides it like a Mustang.
Passion kept her from being responsible.
Now she caught the disease of loneliness.

This story may seem minor
amid tales of congressional investigations
and rape and incest.
But it is about a death.
Not by drowning or by gunshot.
Not even the flashy surface
of a knife.

Three bodies don't fit into a puzzle
It was the death of love.

To Margaret Atwood

I want to feel the pain
want to hurt
want to be.
I want to be trivial.
I will light a candle.
Gigantic nothingness.

Not like Margaret Atwood.
She is alone,
original.
But like Danielle Steele
Out there with the masses.

What would Margaret
Atwood do now,
a gash in her chest
bigger than the
apartment,
the neighborhood,
the world.

Would she go to her
gigantic vocabulary list
to find some words
that would please me.

Would she reach in to her
roll top desk
to find her favorite pen
while I'm reeling from it,
the pain,
that big white finger tip,
the fear that singed my eyelids
that cry.

Don't go.
Margaret hasn't produced
another book yet
and I've already read
Wilderness Tips

In college I told people
I wanted to be a critic.
You don't just be a critic
they said.
You have to have life
experiences.

When does the poem
become more than the event.
He's gone.
Its over now.
I can cease to feel.

He gave me a gift certificate
to the book store
where I saw Margaret Atwood.

Love I

How we fondle love.
Put it in a glass jar.
Carry it around.
Don't touch me.
It might break.
Other people don't count.
They are in the way.
He might call.

And the beginnings
of love are so insecure.
The foot caresses
ever so slightly
the leg
and then the thigh.
The body walks the street
While the mind flirts
with fantasy.

The body flirts
with itself.
It has become more beautiful.
Dressing it is more important.

And what of betrayal.
Treachery.
King Arthur-- courage-- Camelot.
Utopia fallen and scattered
like so many leaves
in the wind.
His castle like so many legos
unattached.

How we fondle love.
Does it matter
For the moment
For the day
For the year.

Passion is no crime.
Remember that.

Love II

I handle all things
delicately.
Touch the taco sauce,
the hamburger,
the frying pan.
What might hurt.

Tiptoe in the bar.
Hold our head high.
Its about to fall.
Be gentle pen.
I hurt.

Tossed around the
seas in a boat wreck
far from shore
if there is one.

I am lost, losing,
a loser in this
relationship.

Its a thin slate of
ice that I cross.
A bottomless pit.
That's how much
Love I need
after 4 years of being
alone.

A tune of waif
Moves me.
My thighs are liquid.
The cafe is home to me.
He plays his voice
like a harp
within my body.

The soft glow of lamps
and fake window panes
make me believe.

Fear glistens,
finding its way
from finger tip
to heart beat.
Lost in the woods
Lost in thought.
And I find that
every move I make
is close to an
explosion of dynamite.

Anticipation.
Fox tracks in the snow.
There is no safe place.
We turn to any God.
I turn to poetry.
It is the only thing
that saves me.
Reaching for that foothold
on the mountain.

To Judy On Her Birthday

The full force of his arm
stung me.
So much blood.
He said grab a
blanket.
So much blood
on the floor of the car,
on my dress.
I thought my nose
was broken.
But he kept driving.
I have to think,
he said.

Upstairs in the
little dormer room
I slept fitfully,
wanting to apologize
for being hit.

Coming Together

It was monumental
and then again
as simple as toast.

After twelve years
I could predict his conversation,
the way he moved.
I watched him with
our son.

He was tall in his suit
with silver hair
that looked expensive.

We went to a book store
that, like our marriage
was out of print.
He bought me two books
on Hemingway.

He said I had a nice dress.
Twenty-five years ago I had
a beautiful body and
was an intellectual.

Once passionate,
we were now neutral
molecules bouncing
off into space.

It was a ceremony,
Justin's graduation,
that brought us
together.

Deep furrows on
his brow scared me.
Thick patches of skin
with deep indentations
like a layout of the brain.

I was the comedian
on my territory,
running the show.

Its only
to see someone
who came across the
country,
who you know so well
is sad.

The Past Is A Song

Being hot and cold
at the same time
is uncomfortable.
From out of the East Coast
where I had my learning
is coming my ex
husband for his
son's graduation.

I'm in perfect health
but my mind trembles.
I rub my knee and
pat it occasionally.

Twelve years since I've
seen that runner,
that professor,
an expert at shaming,
And for 10 years
I said hurt me hurt me
and he did.

In 12 years you can
stop drinking.
You can raise a son,
experience ecstasy.
You can meet so many
men you can't count
them.

You can empty ash-
trays.
Spread the butter
on the toast.
Buy toilet paper.
Raise a child.
Talk about sex.
Do it.

But the past is a
song you have heard
too many times,
a Goddess who has lost
her power.

In the Grocery Store

I   Observe the woman
in the long hair.
Look how she clutches
her basket in front
of her.
What a sense of purpose.
Look how her hands
      are shaking.

II   The soles of my feet
caress the floor.
The sense of touch
is not yet gone.
My breath comes hard.
Asparagus, Chicken
breasts, bread.
Walk the floor.
Hold the basket.
Proceed as if nothing
has happened.
After all it was only
one night of love-
making,
One night of ecstasy,
a 36 hour date
and then two more.

It was only after love
that you dropped
me like a sparrow
into a 30 foot hole
without a word.

III   Cut the asparagus.
The green overlapping
tips remind me of
something.
The chicken is done.
We will have milk
with our dinner.

To Terry On Her Birthday

Crying on your birthday.
Not uncommon.
We mark out these
hideous days to
celebrate when
the human body
just isn't ready.

Your first black
and he shot someone,
went to jail.

Witches all of us
Witches and sisters.

You had two men,
the jail man and your lover.
The man involved
says (in your dreams),
I'm sorry I've
ignored you lately.
Sorry I treat you
like shit.

He's busy.
That's his therapy.
He has time for other women.
Witches and sisters
Talk about it.
Do it.

Comes your birthday

you find out he
shot someone.
Your first black man
like an ink spot
on your white
leather couch.

Right now I'm free of men.
A cloudless sky.
Legs closed tight.
You are a hunter.
Your very brightness
has attracted other
hunters.

So many of us
try to be
both man and woman.
How we always joked
I want a wife.

Baby boom baby,
I never wanted to be
Cinderella. I wanted
to be a Doctor or an
Indian. I saw what
happened to women.

If I could hold you.
If you can just wait
for a simple day,
a nothing day,
not Christmas or Easter.
They are so terrifying,
or Wedding Day,
the worst.

I would lead you
to my day.
It's only food gathering
and reading Rilke's
"Letters to a Young Poet,"
and loving the bark
on the tree and its many
leaves.

Romance

I want to be gathered
from green to red,
droppings from me
like Hailey's Comet.
The color was there
like shooting stars
from an embedded tree.

You are long.
Your are lovely.
Your are lanky.
Your arms glowing
movement.

That was real.
The other was not.
I cannot see myself
like a stuttering typed
monster,
like a failing lover,
like the understatement.

In the room ladies
pass lemon drops-
an uncomfortable pressed
party.
I look over my shoulder
to see you leafing.
Its the edges that are bitter
surrounding me.

Once when I was with you,

you were not there for me.
I watched your face
anyway,
blurs of red
anointing my cheeks.
It was another kind of
crying,
stretched down to receive.

Alone I

Apart or separate.
We are one.
You go and I wait.

I am like a tree
in a parking lot.
Outside I gaze
looking around in despair.

I am like the cat
at 6:30 in the morning.

Alone suddenly.

The cat and I
watch the tree,
sure of the growth
at this minute.

My son will come back soon.
Or I will cry forever.

Alone II

Alone in a hole.
I walk alone.
Tensile fibrous
colorful flowers grow alone.

I observe cheerios, wheaties
in the Uptowner.
On the pink wall
under the blue neon
is a line drawing
of a man and woman.
A map of passion.
Lines can suggest tenderness
more than the human eye.
The eye is the connection.
It is selective,
picks out blue for serenity,
red for passion.

I ramble.
I am grateful for vision.
My mother and grandmother
were blind.
I will be too one day.
What did they think about
without color.

To Georgia O'Keeffe

Sexy flowers.
Colors.
Never a torn petal.
Vaginal lips
in your flowers,
a completeness
never found in nature.

Edges don't exist.
The flowers are pregnant.
You captured the flow,
the ripple,
the cloud-like depth,
the magic run of color blend
that children imagine
that fill the page.

Bonnard Colors

From brain to beast
I will stand up
to your impotence.
You color me with fire
that stops your blood.

Confident beast,
you followed my anger
racing twisting from
yellow to red,
you comforted me.

My hands couldn't
reach you but my
anger would.

Your anger is like my head
where no footprints
will carry that bald
synaptic touch .

I talk with the double
voice of man and beast
There will be no
crouching between us.

Only that some day
we will walk,
when you ready yourself,
eyes glistening
like two ships
culling the water.
I come to you glimmering.

Yellow protects me.
I open up all my organs
to you.

Here is an organ of my
body curled with memory
that a C.A.T. scan cannot
see.

Picasso

What this,
a blackened shadow
sailing across green grass,
abruptly cut off by the fence.

I must return to myself
and cannot resist
looking over the shadow.

So was Picasso as true to
form as the lock of hair,
crazily tearing apart the lines
until they become a shadow,
impulsively holding
the pen to the page.

Let him go.
He is the fence of modern art,
maddeningly dashing off
pictures as if they were
so many leaves in the garden.

Shaping a century with help
from Cocteau, Apollinaire
and Braque and so many
others.
He stood watching with me,
and every time my head moved,
he shot another portrait.

Observation

When does a person
become a poet?
Heart beats that
quicken and slow
quicken and slow
                    the dead
                    the bread
                    the dead.
No, when observing
a tropical plant,
the Dutchman's Pipe.
Splendid imperfection
woven down to meet
the stem.
Came from a small park
South of Tunis.
Probably never planted.

You don't find anorexic
plants.
They all fight to live.

Downtown

We have paved the streets.
Office buildings sit on them.
Slick stone and glass,
some brick.
The Guthrie has banners
and a Caldor mobile.
Balanced acrobats
are the shapes rooted in steel.

Use every minute.
"Ah ah ah ah stayin alive."
Write on the bus.
Write in the restaurant.
Write on the bench.
All things are materials
for your poetry.

Windows and stone.
Windows and steel.
These are our pyramids
where we bury the living.

Skyscraper

Me and Terri on floor 51,
I call her Dr. Atkinson.
Another bar where I drink
Decaf coffee
and Terri struggles with a screwdriver.

All windows and bright lights.
Pathways, former highways,
a tall building in the way.

Severe thunderstorm warnings.
A mist begins blowing
along the windows.
The lights disappear.
The building disappears.

We are in a cloud.
What glorious luck.
All is peach color.
We are filled with wisdom
and importance.
Cups rattle.
People squirm in their chairs.

We trusted this glass edifice.
We are familiar with clouds.
But, now we are part of one
and we come up
gagging for air
suddenly equal.

And we find our leader

in the bartender.
Who has seen this
over and over again.

The Harriet Band Shell

Planes cut the blue sky
like lovers separating.
Cumulus clouds
remain fixed. It is so still.
They turn from fluffy white
to grey with a light in the middle.
Patients coming back from death
report that tunnel and light.

I have come back
To be with the minnows in the lake.
To be with the sky
getting equal for the night.
To step on the weathered board
of the dock, the barn board
in our home in Maine.

Just like the Canadian Brass
with their music stands
and shiny gold crafted instruments,
the band set a little
girl dancing.
She held her skirt up
and turned just right.
The purest sex.

Colored ducks and sailboats,
ruffles, dogs, hats, sandals,
So many greys,
the water, the towers,
and the woman next to me
with a face weathered
like the barn board.

Magical Minnesota.
I have lived in Italy,
England, Boston, Maine
and Illinois.
Minnesota still breaks my heart.

The Minneapolis Chamber Orchestra

With a little pressure
from the bow,
an extension of the hand,
comes music.
It gives me new respect for the arm.
She leans into it
then backs away
absorbed.

I was a musician once.
Piano lessons for eight years.
I was ready to accompany
the McPhail orchestra.
It was in my best interest,
my mother said,
to quit.
A new private school.
Too much to study.

Conductors never change.
They are dancers,
jerking, gyrating
pointing.
I worry about his head
like a mother.
He is the map
of minuets and rondos.

Straus makes me dream.
And it's the first time
I've heard a chamber
orchestra play Joplin.
The rags telling the
story of the
manic depressive.

To Mother

I happened to you.
I have run a thousand
times for and to that smile.
I reached out inside you:
I need to pray.
Reach over.
Reach out.
How can the contrasts
between us become one.
A Mondrion painting
or Klee.

Ten out of ten times
I have loved you.
No words will help me
like you can.
There is my salvation.
I am less and more of you.
I am all and half of you.
The sun baked your smile.
Which part am I.

My Mother's Death

The room awaits me.
A caned chair
covered with white
lace where the cats
scratched.

They are drumming their
feet now into heads and
chests.
They are clutching furious.
Two Siamese
jealous and proud.
They scorn me now.

It was her chair
and I'm glad every day
she is dead.
"Its alright that you are
not pretty dear,
beautiful women have
problems."
So my life was spent,
shamed, criticized
until I hunched
over hiding my face,
far from Oedipus complexes
and I turned to drink.

Artificial Flowers

For four months,
she walked in the cold.
Head bowed.
Braced against the wind.

Until she began to dream.
It was a party
and she was showing off
her house.
Everybody loved the teacups.
When Randy, in her room
held up a china replica
of flowers in a vase.
This is you Judy she said
This is you.

Now Judy had never hated
anything more than
than those sham, make–
believe flowers.
Pretending to be flowers.
Artificial flowers.
Fake flowers.
Counterfeit flowers,
which she only kept in
memory of her mother
and how different they were.

Struggling in the cold
not to be her mother.
Head fiercely tossed
against all her mother's
values,
Against the church.
Against the state.

This is you Judy.
This is you.

Scanning

Another morning.
Cats, coffee, weather,
Headache.
Another morning
when we hear
the results
of magnetic imaging.

Sound of trumpets
for this machine.
It lives in the basement
of Ramsey Hospital.
It makes so much noise
you have to wear ear plugs.

No smoking in this machine.
You can't even wear mascara.
No moving for 30 – 90 minutes.
I take my tylenol #3 with
diet pepsi caffeine free
in a can.

Of course I imagine the worst,
hair shaving, tumors
lesions, an aneurysm,
broken ganglia
in the left hemisphere.

Such silence.
I look at my watch.
It's always the same time.
I look for signs.
The hat, the nude, the family picture.
I check the sky.
Looks like thunder.

Pain

Its like a clenching
in my chest.
It feels deep,
unwanted,
paralyzing.

The brass rubbings stare
down at me,
judgmental,
preserved forever,
all connected with breath.

To feel physically fine,
yet to have something
so wrong, so poisonous,
so strangling.
Pores have opened up.
Foreign elements besiege
me.

Physical pain is easy.
The body doesn't
blame or abandon you.
But this laceration
of love unfulfilled
is throbbing.

Writhing, twisted, tormented,
Let me out of this body.
Get me out of this place,
self contained.

I spoke with philosophers.
Jean Paul Sartre, John Locke.
Logic
doesn't apply to matters
of the heart.
Not even the new
laser methods will work.

Suicide

Thinking of my own death,
I was happy.
This was during hard
times,
when all my friends
were busy,
and my son was going
away to college.

One death,
Like a soldier,
Like an animal in the zoo,
Just one death.
That was Judy.
She ceased to
exist.

Plenty of antidepressants
were available.
No more vision.
No more alone.

The space of death
is a happy place.
It's an escape running
from and not to some place.

Animals die.
Some people bury them.
My father will die soon.
We will burn him.
He is old.
I am old.

This is Judy Manic Depression.
They shoot horses don't they.
She never fit into the world.
She didn't dance.

She didn't smile.
Houses seemed dark.
The colors no longer matched.
It was a clashing apt.
It held a late evening
light.

Crying at the sight of a
McDonald's restaurant.

Singles

Wash away
hurt hurt
Wash away

wash away
hurt hurt
wash away

I got away from the bastard
and into the arms
of someone new.

In the far East,
a woman bowed her head.
Her hair was black and perfect.

One would grunt "talk."
The other talked
and he had something
to say.

Water

A thick dark forest.
A mirror of a lake.
Camp Ajawah,
the camp of 7 birches,
where four developing
young women
trained to swim
the lake and back,
about 6 miles.

For six weeks,
lap after lap,
kick after kick,
til the cartilage
came loose in
my knee causing
me great pain
later in life when
my knee would lock
and the kneecap migrate.

Finally the day came.
The counselors
jumped into the boat
that would follow
us in case of
emergency.
We began to swim
the crawl all the
way.

Stroke breathe

Blow out
Grab for air

My body became cheeks
vibrating.

Stroke breathe
Blow out
Grab for air

It was 3/4 across
that my body disconnected
from my mind.

Glimpses of the other shore
brought Euphoria.
Pride soared.
Self doubt vanished.
I was all powerful.

Only two of us swam back.
We never stopped.
My body was buoyant,
part of the water.

Second wind is
like a birth.
I was the water
and the sky.
I was consciously
unconscious.

No light or tunnel
but fuzziness.
The only separateness
that can be together.

I was no longer swimming.
Something was propelling
me through the water.

Reaching the other side,
my body like jelly,
I watched the other
girl wretch all
over the sand.

Like I was taking
drugs, I was unaware
of the people around me.

My life was my own.

Awakening

I feel a certain
obligation to be famous.
My sister the artist.
My father the Doctor.
My niece the engineer.
My mother the
pillar of the church.

None of them could
have survived
in my three room apartment,
surrounded by my
cactus with its green
knobs like bananas,
clustered together
in a brass container,
or my lamp with
luscious glazes of
red and blue
that challenge stone.

They never would have
cherished the Persian
rug with its primitive
figures on a background
of perfect red.

So I sit on a white
leather couch,
where low self-esteem
is justified,
and condemn

this lack of success
I have had.

Like Anne Sexton,
I tried to kill my self
slowly,
with fifteen years of
alcohol,
and fifteen years of
Navane and Melaril.

Not knowing that
this was death
until I stopped
being sedated,
I was surprised
to wake up one
day and feel things.

The mud painting
stares back at me.
Six birds from Africa.
It was the
obvious that always
gave me trouble.
I tried to leap over it.

Turn around
Turn around
and see art.

To Anne Sexton

To access the unconscious.
To draft a line between
the unknown and the
known in the brain.
That was Anne Sexton's
search for God.

The neurons jump
and play like kittens.
The dendrites
happily send messages
which, when put together
suggest you kill
or not kill,
smile or frown,
live or die.

I have hated
and will hate.
I have sinned
and will sin.

And if, Ann,
there is a God.
He is in your head.
It was peace you
were looking for,
and perfection you
sought.

It was not a journey,
but a lack of movement.
God is sitting
in a bar,
oblivious to the
tragic smell of alcohol
and erupting noise,
people noise.

He started in the womb.
Honor thy father and
mother especially Mary.
And he remains
the most powerful chemical force.

The Counselor

She had a history of
violence at Anoka.
So where was my caution
that night, working
alone in the office,
kneeling on the floor
at the file cabinet.

So when she jumped me
and put her hands
around my neck
trying to strangle me
I hardly knew
what to do.

I'm not a fighter.
Life has never been that
precious to me.
I'll fight for my ego
but not for my life.

It was one mentally
ill person against
another. Only I
was staff and
out of control choking.

She said "Give me
my medication
and I'll let you go."
A wave of thankfull-
ness and prayer

spread over me.

When the police came
they let her have a
cigarette and offered
her a cup of coffee.
They were so careful.

We hold me them
accountable for
our their crimes.

The shaking stopped
when I got home.
I got a week off
and self defense lessons.
They were good to me
there and never knew
I was Manic Depressive.

When I left for good,
they had a roast
and she said,
"She lived with us."

Parenting

I knew my mother
since I was a child.
I mourned her a year ago.

Experts told her
to let the baby cry.
In certain moments
I feel like a baby bird,
mouth gaping open
for a worm. I still can't
fill myself.

My sister tells a story
of one day when my father,
drunk, was shaking my
cradle saying
I want to kill you.
My Doctor says
that is in my memory.

Fort Snelling

Americans all
walk the dusty path.
So much stone
in irregular chunks
of grey and tan.

No one stops the daisies
near the round tower
with its slitted windows.
What better place to be
on the Fourth of July--
little people in the sky.

Dad-- look!
A picture with the guard.
He wears a top hat
with a red pom pom.

This is what made America great.
People on bicycles taking pictures.
Just to be one of them,
macaroni and cheese,
a fence around the yard.

The Lifeless Chair

The chair is wood and gold.
The chair has a woven design.
The chair is pretty.
It has a nice curve.
The chair is old and ugly.

The white lace on the chair
hangs crooked.
The lace is clean.
It was just washed.
I love lace.
I added the lace.
The chair belonged to my
mother before she died.

My Sister

Maybe I had a house in North Oaks.
Maybe the stone steps
led past the sculptures on the lawn.

Maybe my husband
built the pool
surrounded by wild trees,
and natural wood.

Maybe there were birch trees
and bird feeders,
raccoons and deer.

Maybe I found fault
with something.
I doubt it.

They rolled the pool cover out.
The people went up to
the house
designed by the same architect
who designed part of the airport.

Inside the museum house,
besides frescoes, sculptures and carvings,
and the four inch rug,
is a glass vase from Venice,
purple and white perfection.

On Mother's Day

Barnaby and Yannich
are two jealous
siamese cats, the
latter named for a
famous tennis
player by my son.

Barnaby's hair comes
in tufts as smooth
as butter.
His ears, black as
iron filings, lead to
a pure white patch
over his eye,
astounding Mediterranean
blue.
In the middle of his
head are striations
like a walleyes back,
and his browns
are the brown of trench coats,
the brown of toast.
And all the delicate
black hairs of his ear
are more sensible
than eyelashes.

His foot wedged
against my thigh
I feel complete
pregnant again.
He is without imperfection,
like a clear blue sky,
so that to have him
lie on me, to trust me,
is too important
to interrupt
even for a cigarette.

I am his source, the
stream, the deep water
that he swims in,
that gives him nourishment.
Our bellies are one.

They jump to the open
window.
Their litter falls
without disturbing me,
because these will be my children
When my son goes
away to college.
The three of us
wait for him to wake.

Index of First Lines

POEMS OF A MANIC DEPRESSIVE WAS DESIGNED, EDITED AND TYPESET BY RAY HOWE, EDITOR & PUBLISHER, LONE OAK PRESS. THE BOOK WAS SET VIA MICROSOFT WORD FOR WINDOWS ON A LASERMASTER LM1000 PLAIN PAPER TYPESETTER. FONTS ARE FROM THE LASERMASTER FOUNDRY. SCANNING WAS DONE ON A MICROTEK 600Z USING ALDUS PHOTOSTYLER

JUDITH MAIMAN LIVES IN ST. PAUL,
MINNESOTA. SHE HAS HAD PERSONAL
ENCOUNTERS WITH MANIC DEPRESSION.
MAIMAN HAS A MASTER'S DEGREE IN
ART THERAPY AND COUNSELING.

POEMS OF A MANIC DEPRESSIVE IS HER
FIRST PUBLISHED COLLECTION.